羽瀬川 小鷹
Hasegawa Kodaka

A second-year student at Saint Chronica Academy. He looks like a thug. Doesn't have many friends.

三日月 夜空
Mikazuki Yozora

Kodaka's classmate. Other than her looks, she doesn't have much going for her. Doesn't have many friends.

トモちゃん
Tomo-chan

Yozora's "air friend."

羽瀬川 小鳩
Hasegawa Kobato

Kodaka's kid sister. She's a student at Saint Chronica Academy's middle school, and she has some...unfortunate ideas. Her unusual style of clothing and speech stems from her persona as a vampire.

柏崎 星奈
Kashiwazaki Sena

The daughter of Saint Chronica Academy's director. Perfect in every way... except for her personality. Doesn't have many friends.

楠 幸村
Kusunoki Yukimura

A first-year student at Saint Chronica Academy. A kouhai to the rest of the club. Don't be fooled by the maid costume--Yukimura dreams of being a "fine Japanese boy."

志熊 理科
Shiguma Rika

A first-year student at Saint Chronica. She's a genius inventor, and also a perverted yaoi fan who wastes her intelligence.

高山 マリア
Takayama Maria

A ten-year-old girl who wears a nun's habit... and happens to be the Neighbors Club's advisor! She loves both potato chips and Kodaka.

The Neighbors Club
evious club activity logs:
asegawa Kodaka, a lone wolf at a new school, happens to come across his gloomy classmate Mikazuki
ozora chattering happily away by herself. The two of them discuss the process of making friends, and
ozora, who's got energy to spare for the oddest things, spontaneously creates a new club for unfortunate
ouls who desperately need to make friends. More and more students join, and with one exception,
ney're all beautiful--but unfortunate--girls. Next thing you know, the club is up to seven members!
While trying to figure out ways to make friends, the club members play games and put on plays
to entertain themselves, but they always end up
veering wildly off course. But change is
in the air--Yozora's hair caught fire while
the club set off fireworks, and she cut it
short. As the new semester begins,
Kodaka sees her for the first time without
the long hair she took such pride in...
and realizes he knew her long before
"meeting" her at Saint Chronica...
Maria
Club Activity Log 25:
The Beach
The Neighbors Club goes away
on an overnight trip.

Haganai

I don't have many friends

volume 7

ART: ITACHI

STORY: YOMI HIRASAKA

CHARACTER DESIGN: BURIKI

AHH!
IT'S YOUR FAULT!
Club Activity Log 26:
Ghost Stories
At Rika's instigation, the group tells ghost stories.
Club Activity Log 27:
Summer Festival (Part One)
The club heads to the local summer festival as summer break comes to an end.
Club Activity Log 28:
Summer Festival (Part Two)
What better way to mark the end of a festival than fireworks?
SPLASH

Haganai
I don't have many friends

WHAT AM I
SUPPOSED
TO CALL
YOU
NOW...?

IT'S BEEN A WHILE...
TAKA.

Club Activity Log 29:
Reunion

CHATTER
CHATTER
AFTER SCHOOL.
CHATTER
CHATTER

H-
HEY...

WHAT DO YOU WANT?
I WAS JUST WONDERING...
WHAT HAPPENED TO YOUR HAIR?
UH...
I CUT IT.
WELL, YEAH, I CAN SEE THAT.
BUT WHY ALL OF A SUD--
TWITCH
BECAUSE OF WHAT HAPPENED AT THE FESTIVAL.
UGH.

ガッ
SLIDE
ガッ
BUT THAT WAS ONLY THE VERY END, RIGHT?
DON'T YOU THINK YOU OVER-REACTED?
IT'S BECAUSE YOU DUMPED ALL THAT STUFF ON MY HEAD!
I-I'M SO...
IT WOULDN'T COME OUT NO MATTER HOW MUCH I WASHED MY HAIR!
IT SMELLED WEIRD, TOO...
AND IT HURT ...!

I...
I'M SORRY!
LOUD
HONEST, I...
I'M REALLY SORRY.
GRR
......
WELL, WHATEVER.
ON HER HEAD...?

WHISPER
WHISPER
WHISPER

HE EVEN SAID "IT WAS ONLY THE *END*"...
SO HE FORCED HER...
YIKES.

MIKAZUKI PUT UP A FIGHT, SO HE...
HE...
HE *RAPED* HER ...?
THAT'S AWFUL!

ONE SUMMER NIGHT, HE SCREWED UP...
A WEIRD-SMELLING, WHITE LIQUID THAT JUST WOULDN'T COME OFF...
DUMPED ON HER...
!!

Y-
YOU'VE GOT IT ALL WRONG!
GLARE
AND WHO SAID IT WAS "WHITE" ...?!
MEEP!
GRAB
C'MON.
THIS WAY!
AH!
HEY! WAIT!
CLAMOR
CLAMOR
SLAM

HUFF
HUFF
WE SHOULD BE OKAY OUT HERE.
YANK
GAH... EVERYONE'S GOT THE WRONG IDEA AGAIN.
HMPH.
THAT DOESN'T MATTER.
UM, YEAH, ACTUALLY IT DOES!

STARE
NO, THE IMPORTANT THING IS--
IS... WHAT?
?
ERR...
UH...
THE IMPORTANT THING IS...
OH, YOU KNOW ...!
WHAT I'M TRYING TO SAY IS...

I WAS SORA ALL ALONG!!

DON'T YOU HAVE ANYTHING TO SAY?!

......
UH...

......
I WAS COMPLETELY SURPRISED!
......
I-ISN'T THERE ANYTHING ELSE...?
ANYTHING ELSE...?
ON THE VERGE OF TEARS.
W-WELL, LIKE...
LIKE YOU'RE HAPPY... OR HONORED...
OR YOU'RE DEEPLY TOUCHED...
THERE'S NO POINT SAYING ANY OF THAT.
HUH?
IT'S LIKE...
I DON'T EVEN KNOW WHERE TO START.
THERE'S A TON OF THINGS I WANT TO ASK...

BUT YEAH, BEING TOTALLY SURPRISED...
IS WHAT I'M FEELING MOST RIGHT NOW.

TMP
TMP
BY THE WAY...
THAT HAIRCUT LOOKS PRETTY GOOD ON YOU.
HUH?
D-DON'T ...!
I...
I WENT TO A HAIR SALON FOR A CHANGE.
A SALON?
THAT'S RIGHT.
THIS STYLE I GOT IS EVEN POPULAR RIGHT NOW.
IT'S CALLED... UM...
JAGI, MAYBE ...?
YEEHAW! SAY MY NAME, BITCHES!
UH... SHAGGY?
YEAH, THAT!

TMP
THE STYLIST KEPT MOUTHING OFF AT ME...
ABOUT WHAT A SHAME IT WAS "TO CHOP OFF SUCH BEAUTIFUL HAIR."
TMP
BUT I ADMIT SHE DID A GREAT JOB ON IT.
......

SO...
HOW LONG...
HAVE YOU KNOWN THAT I WAS TAKA?
...
UM?

I KNEW RIGHT AWAY.
WHO CARES?

RIGHT AWAY?!

I... THINK I'M STARTING TO GET IT.
COME ON, LOOK AT YOUR HAIR! OF COURSE I KNEW!
I CAN'T REALLY ARGUE WITH THAT.

WAIT. BUT THEN...
WHY'D YOU ACT LIKE YOU DIDN'T KNOW ME WHEN WE FIRST TALKED?

WELL, SINCE I REMEMBERED...
I WAS KINDA OFFENDED THAT YOU DIDN'T.

SO YOU PLAYED DUMB.
THAT'S RIGHT.
WELL... SORRY ABOUT THAT.
BUT IT'S NOT MY FAULT, YOU KNOW.
I MEAN, I'D ALWAYS THOUGHT THAT...
YOU WERE A BOY.
......
I DON'T RECALL EVER SAYING I WAS.
BUT YOU LOOKED AND SOUNDED LIKE A BOY.
AND WHO'D EXPECT A KID WHO JUMPED INTO FIGHTS LIKE THAT TO BE A GIRL?
CREAK

YOU'RE THE ONE WHO UP AND DISAPPEARED BEFORE I TOLD YOU I WAS A GIRL.

"HEY, TAKA? I'VE GOTTA TELL YOU SOMETHING REALLY IMPORTANT TOMORROW."
WAS THAT THE "REALLY IMPORTANT" THING YOU WERE GOING TO TELL ME...?
......
NOD
HANG ON, THOUGH.
YOU'RE THE ONE WHO DIDN'T SHOW UP THAT DAY.
WELL...
ER...
CLENCH
IT'S JUST ...
......

IT WAS TOO EMBAR-RASSING!
HAVING YOU SEE ME IN A...
A...
IN A SKIRT!
......
SKIRT?
SULK

WHAT I'M SAYING IS...
THAT DAY, I PUT ON NORMAL "GIRL" CLOTHES...
SO YOU'D KNOW I WAS A GIRL!
BUT BACK THEN, I'D NEVER WORN A SKIRT IN MY LIFE...
SO I COULDN'T TELL IF I LOOKED RIDICULOUS!
I THOUGHT YOU MIGHT LAUGH AT ME!

IF I'D KNOWN YOU WERE MOVING AWAY THAT DAY...
CLENCH
SNIFF

SO IT'S YOUR FAULT!
GRRR!
I AUTO-MATICALLY SNAPPED BACK LIKE IT WAS A JOKE...
ACK!
HOW'S IT MY FAULT ?!
WIPE
WIPE

ANYWAY ...
YOU'VE COULD'VE JUST TOLD ME. YOU DIDN'T NEED TO WEAR A SKIRT.
HMPH.
I FIGURED YOU WERE SUCH A BLOCKHEAD THAT...
YOU WOULDN'T BELIEVE ME IF I JUST SAID I WAS A GIRL.
I... GUESS SHE'S GOT A POINT THERE.
I'M A GIRL!
WHAT ?!
STRIP
SHE WOULD'VE NEEDED TO DO THAT...

ANYWAY, LISTEN.
DON'T TELL THE REST OF THE CLUB...
THAT YOU AND I WERE FRI--
THAT WE KNEW EACH OTHER AS KIDS.
HMM?
......
WHY NOT?
IT'S NOT REALLY SOMETHING YOU SHOULD FLAUNT AT THEM, IS IT?
WELL ...
SURE, I GUESS.

YEAH.
GLAD YOU UNDERSTAND.
HURRY UP!
OH!
THERE'S ONE THING--
?

WHAT AM I...
SUPPOSED TO CALL YOU NOW?
Common Room 4
......
WHAT'S THE MATTER?
N-
NOTHING AT ALL!

ガ
OPEN
チャ
WHAT'S UP, GUYS?
OH, KODAKA-SEMPAI!
CLACK
GOOD AFT...
?
......

OMG!!! A SCANDALOUS PHOTO OF KODAKA-SEMPAI WITH A MYSTERIOUS PRETTY BOY--!!!
Yes!
HUH?
"PRETTY BOY"?

ZOOM
WHO...
WHO...
WHO...
WHO, IF RIKA MAY ASK, IS THAT DARLING PRETTY BOY, SEMPAI?!!
UHH... WHAT PRETTY BOY?
NO, WAIT!
KINDLY BELAY YOUR ANSWER, IF YOU WOULD!
RIKA WILL DISPLAY HER POWERS OF DEDUCTION!
BAM
1. KODAKA-SEMPAI'S KOUHAI!
2. KODAKA-SEMPAI'S SEMPAI!
3. KODAKA-SEMPAI'S LITTLE BROTHER!
4. KODAKA-SEMPAI'S FIANCÉ!
5. KODAKA-SEMPAI'S RIVAL ON THE SOCCER TEAM!
WRONG.
A-ANIKI AND...
TREMBLE
A...A PRETTY BOY...?
......

WHICH ONE IS THE UKE? WHICH IS THE SEME...?
ROLL
ROLL
THE MERE THOUGHT IS ENOUGH TO MAKE RIKA...!
MAKE RIKA... OOOOOOH!!!
ROLL
ROLL
DAMN PERVERT...
AHHHHHHHHHH~!
SHE'S HOPELESS...
CLICK
OH, HEY, YOZORA.
YOU CUT YOUR HAIR?

WHAT?
YOZORA-SEMPAI?
PLOP
FLUTTER

THE WAY I LOOK SHOULD SAY IT ALL...
MEAT.
HMPH!

STEp
Examine
Examine
YOU LOPPED IT ALL OFF, HUH?
WHY'D YOU GO AND DO THAT?
C'MON...
YOU CAN TELL LITTLE OLD ME!
WHAT'S IT TO YOU...?
IGNORE
HEY!
ANSWER ME!
STOP TALKING TO ME.
TALKING TO YOU MAKES IT HARDER FOR ME TO HAVE A SATISFYING OFFLINE LIFE.
HOW DOES TALKING TO ME DO THAT?!
OH.
SNAp

HEE HEE! ♪
GLEAM
TWITCH
...!
MAYBE SOME-BODY'S NURSING A BROKEN HEART?
A-HA! DID I HIT A BULLS-EYE?
HUH? WHY WOULD SHE...?
YOU REALLY ARE HEART-BROKEN?!
HA HA HA HA!
MOOOO-RON!
TWIRL
TWIRL
YOZORA GOT DUMPED!
YOU'RE SO PATHETIC!!
TWIRL

UNISHMENT
BWAH --?!

OWWWWWWW...
UNFORTUNATELY FOR YOU...
MY HEART'S PERFECTLY INTACT.
HOWEVER ...

YOU JUST DEMONSTRATED HOW YOU'D ACT IF I WERE ACTUALLY GOING THROUGH EMOTIONAL TRAUMA!

WHAT'S YOUR DEAL ...?
AND HERE I THOUGHT I FINALLY HAD A CHANCE TO BULLY YOU...

YAP
BUT IF THAT'S NOT IT, THEN WHY?
YAP
YAP
I'M NOT TELLING.
OH, COME ON. TELL ME!
OH, THAT'S RIGHT!
RUSTLE
UM...
YOZORA-SEMPAI!
VOILA
PLEASE PUT THIS ON...!
WH-WHAT THE HECK IS THAT?

THIS GLORIOUS WHITE JACKET HAS THE **HONOR** OF BEING WORN ONLY BY **PRESIDENTS** OF THE STUDENT COUNCIL AT **TEIRITSU GALFORD ACADEMY!**
WHERE'S THAT...?

AND WHY DO *YOU* HAVE IT?

CUTE ROUND EYES!
RIKA GOT IT FROM A VIDEO GAME COMPANY EMPLOYEE!

GAME...
SO THAT'S FOR **COSPLAY?**
WHY THE HELL WOULD I DO ***COSPLAY*** ?!!

BE-CAUSE YOU'D LOOK *GREAT!*
RIKA IS ABSO-LUTELY *POSITIVE* YOU'D LOOK DASHING!

HMM...

PLEEEEEEEEEEEASE?!

BAM

YOU'D LOOK SOO-OOO-OOO-OOO-OOO DASHING IN IT!

OMG!!! A PIC OF THE STUDENT COUNCIL PRESIDENT WITH A THUG!!!!!
WHO'RE YOU CALLING A THUG?
EXCUSE ME? "STUDENT COUNCIL PRESIDENT"?
HMPH ...
Y-YOU DON'T LOOK HALF BAD IN THAT.
I HAVE NO IDEA WHAT'S WHAT ANYMORE ...
DO I REALLY LOOK GOOD LIKE THIS...?

TURN AWAY
AHHHHH! RIKA CAN'T TAKE IT! SHE JUST CAN'T TAKE IT!!
ONII-CHAN! ONII-CHAN!
BAM

HUH?
?
WHAT'S THE MATTER?
TAKING A POOP?
HIT BY THE DOOR.
YOU'RE AS BOUNCY AS ALWAYS...
MARIA.

AH!
ONII-CHAN! ONII-CHAN!
GUESS WHAT! GUESS WHAT!
TODAY, I--
PALING
P...
PRETTY... BOY....
THERE'S A S-SUPER... PRETTY... BOY...!
WHAT?
WHAT'RE YOU SO SCARED OF?
COWER

HAVEN'T YOU HEARD, ONII-CHAN?!
PRETTY BOYS ARE SOOOOO SCARY!
THEY GOBBLE ADORABLE GIRLS RIGHT UP--!
AND I'M SUPER-CUTE SO I HAVE TO BE ON GUARD AROUND THEM...!
P:YO!!
THAT'S WHAT THE OLD HAG TOLD ME!
UH... WHAT OLD HAG?
MARIA'S GUARDIAN, MAYBE...?
HA HA HA HA!
BUT DON'T WORRY, ONIICHAN! THERE'S NO WAY YOU COULD BE A PRETTY BOY!
OH, REALLY? THANKS.
SMOOTH
I AM PRETTY-BOY.
I SHALL...
SWALLOW YOU WHOLE.
GYAAAAAAAAAAA!!!

WHAT ABOUT YUKIMURA? I BET HE'S DELICIOUS!
UH... YUKI-MURA'S KIND OF A SPECIAL CASE.
NO, LITTLE GIRLS ARE MY FAVORITE SNACK!
GAH!
GAH!

SHEESH... IT'S NICE OF HER TO FINALLY PUT IN AN APPEARANCE.
BUT NO MATTER HOW LONG HER HAIR IS...
YOZORA'S STILL YOZORA.
...

......

WHAT AM I
SUPPOSED TO CALL
YOU NOW?

"YOZORA."

JUST KEEP CALLING ME...
YOZORA.
"ONLY FRIENDS ARE SUPPOSED TO USE NICKNAMES."

ONCE UPON A TIME, THERE WERE TWO FRIENDS NAMED TAKA AND SORA.
BUT...
THAT DOESN'T MEAN HASEGAWA KODAKA AND MIKAZUKI YOZORA HAVE THE SAME RELATIONSHIP.
IT SHOULD HAVE BEEN OBVIOUS THAT...
REALIZING THAT YOZORA AND SORA WERE THE SAME PERSON...
WOULDN'T MAGICALLY RESTORE THE FRIENDSHIP KODAKA HAD WITH HER TEN YEARS AGO.

NO MATTER HOW LONG HER HAIR IS...
YOZORA'S STILL YOZORA.

YEAH, THAT'S TRUE.

SENA WAS THE ONE WHO UNDER-STOOD...
THAT YOZORA WAS STILL HERSELF, NO MATTER HOW LONG HER HAIR WAS.
WHAT'S WITH YOU?
UH, NOTHING.
Common Room 4
OKAY, THEN.
WHAT'S ON THE CLUB AGENDA FOR TODAY...?

To tell the truth...

AFTER RIKA HAD HER WAY WITH YOZORA...
YOU ROCK, YOZORA-SEMPAI!
TRY THIS ON NEXT!
NO!
Room 4

GASP GASP
HUH. YOU'RE A PUSH-OVER AROUND RIKA.
A HUGE ONE.

HOW THE HELL DO I DEAL WITH SOMEONE WHO DOESN'T CARE IF YOU YELL AT HER OR HIT HER?!
I GUESS THERE'RE SOME PEOPLE NOT EVEN YOZORA CAN STEAMROLL.

Haganai
I don't have many friends

ALL DONE!!
WELL, KODAKA?
DOES IT SUIT ME?
YEAH.
IT SUITS YOU PERFECTLY.

I Don't

Have

Many

Club Activity Log 30: Pouf

Friends

AND LIFT!
CLATTER
PHEW!
THE FIRST WEEK OF SEPTEMBER.
IN ORDER TO CRAM MORE STUFF INTO OUR SPACE...
WE REARRANGED THE CLUB ROOM A LITTLE.

IT FEELS MORE CHAOTIC IN HERE ALL THE TIME...
BUT THAT WAS ONLY THE FIRST HINT OF THE TRAGEDY TO COME.

WHEW...
TWIRL TWIRL
Cast Member:
Mikazuki Yozora
Leading Role:
Kashiwazaki Sena
HMM...
WHY'RE YOU STARING INTO SPACE?
HUH?

I WAS WONDERING IF MAYBE I SHOULD CUT MY HAIR, TOO.
HUH?
YOU TOO?

......

DON'T COPY ME, MEAT.
HEY!
WHO'D TRY TO COPY YOU?!
I JUST THOUGHT I'D CHANGE IT UP A BIT! I'M TIRED OF THIS STYLE!
HMPH!
CREAK
ACTUALLY, THAT REMINDS ME. I LEARNED SOMETHING FASCINATING ABOUT HAIRSTYLES WHEN I GOT MINE CUT.
SOMETHING FASCINATING?
I'M IN A GOOD MOOD, SO I'LL TELL YOU.
I READ IT IN A MAGAZINE ...
AT THE HAIR SALON.

THESE DAYS, A LOT OF BIG-CITY WOMEN WITH HAPPY LIVES...
ARE WEARING A NEW STYLE CALLED A "POUF."
POUF?
AH!
SLAM
IT'S A MODERN-DAY SUCCESSOR TO THE ARISTOCRATIC STYLES FROM THE MIDDLE AGES...!
BELIEVE IT OR NOT, THEY EVEN INCLUDED SUCH THINGS AS *THIS.*
WHAT THE HELL...? IS SHE A GENERAL FROM THE WARRING STATES PERIOD*?
IT'S QUITE UNIQUE AND BEAUTI-FUL.
WELL, SETTING ASIDE ITS *FUNCTION,* YOU COULD MAKE A CASE FOR THAT...
IN THE SENSE THAT IT'S INTENDED TO EXHIBIT ONE'S *INDIVIDUALITY.*

The Sengoku Period (mid 15th century to 17th century) was a time social upheaval, political intrigue, and near-constant conflict.

HMM...
I SEE.
I'M NOT SURE I GET IT, BUT IT LOOKS LIKE YOU'D HAVE TO BE *CRAZY* TO TRY IT.
I SUPPOSE YOU COULD SAY THAT.
LOWER-CLASS WOMEN...
TWITCH
COULD *NEVER* PULL OFF THE "POUF" STYLE!
IT WOULD BE RECKLESS...
FOR A COMMONER TO EVEN ATTEMPT IT.
IF AN AVERAGE GIRL...
WANTED TO GET A NEW HAIRSTYLE...
SHE'D GO TO A NORMAL SALON LIKE EVERYONE ELSE.
THAT'D BE THE SAFEST MOVE, OBVIOUSLY.

BUT I SURE WOULD LIKE TO SEE A POUF IN PERSON JUST ONCE IN MY LIFE...
RIKA QUITE AGREES. WITH YOUR OLD HAIR, YOU MIGHT HAVE BEEN ABLE TO PULL OFF THE POUF STYLE BEAUTIFULLY.
SIGH ...
IS THERE NO ONE WITH A REFINED, GORGEOUS AIR ABOUT HER...?
A BORN NOBLE-WOMAN WHO CAN MASTER EVEN THE FLAMBOYANT SELF-EXPRESSION OF THE POUF?
HA HA HA! COME NOW, YOZORA-SEMPAI.
SUCH REFINED LADIES ONLY EXIST IN ANIME AND MANGA.
WHO THE HELL WOULD FALL FOR SOMETHING THIS OBVIOUS...?
HA HA HA HA!

BAM
COME OFF IT, GUYS!
SHE'S RIGHT IN FRONT OF YOU!
YOU'VE GOT YOURSELVES A REFINED LADY EXUDING HER GORGEOUS AURA ALL OVER YOU!
SMIRK

HA HA!
THERE'S NO WAY, MEAT.
IT'S TRUE.
YOU MIGHT BE ABLE TO WEAR IT, BUT HARDLY ANYONE CAN MAKE IT A SUCCESS!
I'LL NEVER KNOW UNLESS I TRY!
OH, GOSH, NO.
BAM
I CAN TELL. YOU DON'T NEED TO TRY.
PUT MY HAIR UP...
WHAM
IN ONE OF THESE "POUF" THINGS!
GRIN
RIGHT. OF COURSE SENA TOOK THE BAIT.
SMILE

AND SO THE PROJECT WAS UNDERWAY...

FWISH
BRUSH
BRUSH
BRUSH
BRUSH
BRUSH
BRUSH
BRUSH

SIGH...!
YOUR HAIR'S SO SILKY, SENA-SEMPAI.
NOT A SINGLE SPLIT END.
WELL, THIS IS MY HAIR WE'RE TALKING ABOUT!
THIS MAY BE THE ONLY COMPLIMENT I EVER GIVE YOU, BUT YOU DO HAVE BEAUTIFUL HAIR.
MUCH AS I HATE TO ADMIT IT...
BUT, YOZORA-SEMPAI...
YOUR HAIR'S GORGEOUS TOO. RIKA'S JEALOUS.
THAT'S TRUE. I CAN COMPLIMENT YOU ON YOUR HAIR.
BUT THAT'S ALL.
BUT, HEY, YOUR HAIR'S PRETTY AND SHINY TOO, RIKA.
HUH? REALLY?
YEAH!

EVERY ONCE IN A WHILE...
I WISH I HAD BLACK HAIR LIKE YOU TWO.
ON THE SAME NOTE, RIKA WISHES SHE HAD BLONDE HAIR LIKE YOU, SENA-SEMPAI.
I SUPPOSE ...
I FEEL THAT WAY EVERY ONCE IN A WHILE TOO.
HEE HEE!
GIGGLE

I CAN'T INTRUDE ON THEIR BONDING MOMENT...
YOUR TEA.
CAREFUL, IT'S HOT.
CLACK
ALL RIGHT.

IT'S FINALLY TIME TO POUF IT UP!
FLIP
INDEED!
MEAT!
DO YOU HAVE ANY REQUESTS?
HMM...
盛り髪カタログ

I'M NOT SURE HOW IT WORKS, EXACTLY.
COULD YOU GIVE IT THE FEEL OF THOSE WOMEN WITH THEIR HAPPY LIVES?
SO THE THEME IS PEOPLE WHO ENJOY THEIR REAL-WORLD LIVES...
LET'S SEE.

WHAT THAT BRINGS TO MIND IS...
SUMMER, I THINK?
AH! GREAT IDEA, YOZORA-SEMPAI!
POP
THE AIR OF A HAPPY PERSON LIVING LIFE TO THE FULLEST IN THE SUMMER!
NOW, WE'LL BEGIN BY EVOKING THE EBB AND FLOW OF WAVES AT THE SEASHORE...
RUSTLE
DOING THE SAME THING OVER THE WHOLE HEAD ISN'T UNIQUE.
LET'S THROW IN SOME RINGLETS TO ADD AN ACCENT OF WHIRLPOOL IMAGERY!
OOOH, VERY NICE. ♪
WH-WHIRLPOOL?!

HEE-YAH!
PSYCHO CRUSHER!
SPLAT
GEL
?!
AH--! THE LACK OF EQUILIBRIUM IS EXQUISITE!
DON'T YOU THINK SO, SENA-SEMPAI?
POP
AGREED!
GLEAM
GLEAM
SLURP
SLURP
SLURP
UH, YEAH ...
SOUNDS GOOD...

ALL RIGHT!
LET'S TACKLE THE TOP!
WON'T BE NEEDING THIS.
TOSS
WE'VE GOT A GREAT OCEAN ON THE SIDE...
SO HOW ABOUT A POUF EVOKING A SAND-CASTLE?!
THAT SOUNDS MARVEL-OUS!
HUH?
A CASTLE WOULD BE IN LINE WITH SENA-SEMPAI'S REGAL (LOL) STYLE!
AH! THAT'S GREAT!
WHAT IF WE USE A BIKINI INSTEAD OF A RIBBON?
SLURP SLURP SLURP
WOW! YOU REALLY ARE A GENIUS!
AND SOME WATER-MELON AND FIRE-WORKS WOULD BE NICE...!
AND A DAY AT THE BEACH ABSOLUTELY CALLS FOR YAKISOBA! OR CURRY!
YES! NOW WE'VE GOT A FULL-FLEDGED GIRL HAPPY WITH HER OFFLINE LIFE!
......

JOLT
ALL RIGHT! LET'S ADORN THE WAVES WITH SOME YAKISOBA!
Y-YAKI-SOBA...?!
YUKI-MURA-KUN!
GO BUY SOME YAKISOBA, A BIKINI, A WATER-MELON, AND SOME FIREWORKS!
CATCH
YOUR WISH IS MY COMMAND.
H-HELP ME, KODAKA!
I'M SO SORRY.
CLANG
CLANG
AT LAST, THE FATEFUL MOMENT ARRIVED.

ALL DONE !!
THE ULTIMATE MID-SUMMER NIGHT'S DREAM...
AH...
SO PRETTY.

ど
VOILA
MEGA MAX POUF FOR A HAPPY REAL-WORLD GIRL!!
YEAH!

※THERE IS NO BULLYING IN THIS CLUB.
YOU'RE SO CUTE, SENA-SEMPAI! ♡
GRILLED SQUID
CICADA HUSK (YUKIMURA FOUND IT ON THE GROUND)
FIREWORKS
MELON BREAD (IN LIEU OF WATERMELON)
AH! SO CUTE!
YOU'RE SO, SOOOOOO CUTE--!
DRAGONFLY CORPSE (YUKIMURA FOUND IT ON THE GROUND)
BIKINI
UGH! I CAN'T BELIEVE I WASTED ALL THAT HAIR!
FREAKING OUT
CASTLE
I SHOULD'VE TRIED THE POUF BEFORE GETTING MY HAIR CUT OFF!
......
......
DO...
DO I REALLY LOOK THAT GOOD...?
YAKISOBA

OH, IT JUST LOOKS SO AMAZING ON YOU, SEMPAI! ♪
CLICK
YEAH.
I HATE TO ADMIT IT, BUT YOU LOOK GOOD!
DAMMIT!
I SENSE THE FLEETING LIVES OF THE CICADA AND DRAGON-FLY...
?
AND A POIGNANT WISTFUL-NESS FOR THE TRAN-SIENCE OF BEAUTY.
MM...
MMM...
MWA HA!
THIS REALLY...
DOES SEEM PRETTY GREAT...
YAY!
HOW DO I LOOK?
WHAT DO YOU THINK, KODAKA?
WHA?
HOW THE HELL IS THIS HAPPENING?!
......
IT PRACTICALLY SCREAMS "SENA."
I KNOW, RIGHT?! ♪
PAT

IT EMBODIES HOW UNFORTUNATE YOU ARE.
HEE HEE!
FOR REAL?
THAT NIGHT, SENA WENT HOME WEARING "THE ULTIMATE MIDSUMMER NIGHT'S DREAM MEGA MAX POUF FOR A HAPPY REAL-WORLD GIRL!!" HAIR.
THE NEXT DAY.

......
MORNING ...
HEY...
SNIFF...
PAPA GOT REALLY MAD AT ME WHEN I GOT HOME YESTERDAY.
HE SPANKED ME AND MADE ME PUT MY HAIR BACK THE WAY IT WAS. IT WAS SO TRAUMATIC...
AFTER I GOT RIKA AND YOZORA TO DO ALL THAT WORK ON IT...
GOOD JOB, PEGASUS-SAN!

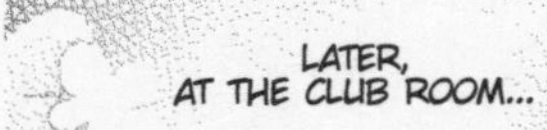
LATER, AT THE CLUB ROOM...

UH... WE...
WE WENT A BIT TOO FAR. WE GOT CARRIED AWAY.
SORRY ABOUT THAT.
RIKA APOLOGIZES AS WELL.
YOU COULD AT LEAST END WITH THE JOKE!

RIP PUNCHLINE
GOOD JOB, PEGASUS-SAN!

AFTER SCHOOL ...
IN THE CLUB ROOM ...
Club Activity Log 31:
Yaoi Game Club
THERE WAS A GIRL I'D NEVER SEEN BEFORE.

STARE
......
?

OH, IT'S JUST YOU, RIKA.
YOU CONFUSED ME FOR A SECOND.
WHAT ?!
SHUT
THE FIRST THING YOU DO WHEN YOU ARRIVE IS ANNOUNCE THAT RIKA HAS DISAP-POINTED YOU?!
SO...
WHERE'D YOUR GLASSES GO?
CREAK
RIKA DIDN'T BRING THEM TODAY.
FROM TIME TO TIME, SHE DOESN'T FEEL LIKE WEARING THEM.
THAT'S HOW ONE GOES ABOUT CHANGING ONE'S IMAGE.
YOU DON'T FEEL LIKE WEARING THEM...?

SO YOU'VE GOT CONTACTS IN?
OH, NO. RIKA'S GLASSES ARE ENTIRELY FOR SHOW.
ARE YOU SERIOUS?!!
YES.
AS IT HAPPENS, RIKA HAS EXCELLENT EYESIGHT.
BUT... WHY WOULD YOU WEAR GLASSES FOR *SHOW*?
ISN'T "FOR SHOW" SELF-EXPLANATORY?
CLEARLY, RIKA DOES IT AS A *FASHION STATEMENT*.
I NEVER IMAGINED HEARING THE WORDS "FASHION STATEMENT" COME OUT OF YOUR MOUTH.
IF A CHARACTER'S TRADEMARK IS GLASSES...
THE GLASSES AREN'T SUPPOSED TO COME OFF...!
SIGH...

SO...
HOW DOES RIKA LOOK WITHOUT THEM?
PEER
UHHHH, WHAT DO YOU MEAN...?

......

SHE'S NOT LIKE YOZORA BEFORE SHE CUT HER HAIR...
WITH THE "COOL AND COLLECTED BEAUTY" THING GOING ON.
AND SHE'S NOT LIKE SENA, WHO'S SO GORGEOUS SHE TURNS HEADS.

THEY'RE BOTH SO PERFECT THAT THEY'RE UNAPPROACHABLE.
RIKA'S JUST CUTE, IN AN ACCESSIBLE, FRIENDLY-LOOKING WAY.
IF I WANTED TO MAKE SOME KIND OF POETIC COMPARISON, I'D SAY IT'S LIKE HOW A SINGLE FLOWER ON A HILLSIDE IS PRECIOUS.
AS FOR WHETHER IT'S SOMETHING I'M INTO...
AS FOR WHETHER IT'S SOMETHING I'M INTO...
TO BE HONEST, IT'S RIGHT UP MY ALLEY.

WH...
WH-WH-WH-WHY WOULD YOU COME RIGHT OUT WITH THAT...
SEMPAI?!
HUH...?
ER... DID I SAY THAT OUT LOUD?
LOUD AND CRYSTAL CLEAR!
HUH?
BLUSH
?
?
?
I GUESS SHE'S A LITTLE SHY ABOUT IT...?

……
WHAT'S WRONG, YOZORA?
OH, NOTHING.
……
SHUT
WHAT THE...?

THAT SAID...
RIKA HAD NO IDEA YOU WERE SO DRAWN TO HER, KODAKA-SEMPAI!
LET'S CELEBRATE BY DOING SOMETHING DIRTY, SEMPAI!
FWIP
RIGHT NOW!
WHAT IS WRONG WITH YOU?!
UGH.
SHE'S BACK TO NORMAL.
YOU'RE RIGHT.
AHEM!
WHERE ARE RIKA'S MANNERS? THAT WAS TOO CRASS.
RIKA WILL ASK POLITELY.
WOULD YOU CARE TO PERFORM DIRTY ACTS WITH RIKA...
SLOUCH
SEMPAI?
GUUUUUUH.

WHY... WHY DO YOU HAVE TO BE RIKA...?
IF ONLY YOU WEREN'T RIKA...
IS THERE NO GOD WHO PRESIDES OVER SEX?
YOU'RE GOING TO REJECT RIKA AS A PERSON WITH THAT LOOK ON YOUR FACE?!
RIKA'S THE ONE WHO SHOULD BE CRYING!!!
IT HURTS SO GOOD.
I KNOW I'M REPEATING MYSELF, BUT PHYSICALLY, SHE'S EXACTLY MY TYPE.
AWW. ALL RIGHT.
RIKA WILL ESCAPE TO THE SECOND DIMENSION TO SALVE HER HEART.
CLATTER
I'LL DO HOMEWORK.
SENA-SEMPAI, MIGHT RIKA USE THE TV?
WHY WON'T YOU DIE?!
HUH? OH, SURE.

YOU PLAYING A GAME?
RIKA'S GOING TO WATCH SOME ANIME.
RIKA GOT THE BLU-RAY FROM AMAZONES YESTERDAY.
CLACK
WHAT ANIME?
GLEAM
YAOI GAME CLUB: THE MOTION PICTURE.

WHAP
HOW DARE YOU TRY TO SHOW INDECENT MATERIAL IN HERE--!
YOU DEVI-ANT!
OWW!
YOU'VE HEARD OF IT?
SEETHE
NO, I HAVE NOT HEARD OF IT!
BUT I'M STILL 100% SURE IT'S YOU-KNOW-WHAT FROM THE TITLE!
TRUE ENOUGH.
IT IS NOT INDECENT!
SEE WHAT IT'S MISSING?!
EEEEEEK!
DON'T SHOW IT OFF, MORON!
ホモゲ部
Yaoi Game Club
HEAR RIKA OUT!
TAKE A GOOD, HARD LOOK!
THERE'S NO "18+ ONLY" LABEL!!!
TA-DA!

COME ON! JUST TAKE A LOOK!
SHOVE
SEE?!
SHOVE
STOP!
WHETHER IT'S RESTRICTED OR NOT...
WITH A COVER AND TITLE LIKE THAT...
THERE'S NO WAY IT CAN BE A DECENT ANIME!
HOW CAN YOU SAY THAT WITHOUT EVEN WATCHING IT?!
RIKA FEELS IT'S UNFAIR TO JUDGE A BLU-RAY BY ITS COVER!
I...
I SAID, KEEP THAT AWAY FROM ME!

WHAM
SHE'S RIGHT.
BACK THEN-- LIKE NOW-- MY LOOKS MADE ME STAND OUT.
AND THAT MEANT I GOT BULLIED.
SHE'S RIGHT.
I DON'T THINK IT'S FAIR TO JUDGE SOMETHING BY THE WAY IT LOOKS.
STAND
KODAKA-SEMPAI...!
KODAKA--!
IF YOU'RE GOING TO REJECT SOMETHING...
YOU SHOULD DO IT *AFTER* YOU'VE TAKEN A LOOK AT WHAT'S INSIDE.
BEING REJECTED BECAUSE OF HOW YOU LOOK...
IS PRETTY ROUGH.

GRR...
FINE, KODAKA. IF THAT'S HOW YOU FEEL.
THAT'S KODAKA-SEMPAI FOR YOU!
LET'S ALL WATCH *YAOI GAME CLUB* TOGETHER, YOZORA-SEMPAI!
RIKA THINKS THAT EVEN AS A NEWCOMER, YOU'LL FIND THE CONTENT ACCEPTABLE!
......
UGH, WHY DO I HAVE TO DO THIS...?
NOW, NOW, DON'T BE THAT WAY.
RIKA IS **CONFIDENT** THAT YOUR HEART WILL BE STIRRED...
BY THE **BEAUTIFUL FRIENDSHIP** BETWEEN THESE MEN. *HEE!*

BEAUTIFUL FRIENDSHIP...
FIX YOUR TIE, WILL YOU?
OH!

AND SO IT CAME TO PASS...

AND NOW, OUR SCREENING OF...
YAOI GAME CLUB...
劇場版
ホモゲ部
HE'S REGRETTING THIS A BIT.
Yaoi Game Club:
The Motion Pict
*Cover

BAM
YAOI GAME CLUB THE MOTION PICTURE - OUR TRUE FORTUNE
DAT DA DA DAA
CAN BEGIN!
GULP

KI
BIIING
BOOONG
HI, I'M KUSAKABE FUMIO-- JUST YOUR DEAD AVERAGE HIGH SCHOOL STUDENT.
MY ORIGINAL PLAN WAS TO JOIN THE FOOTBALL TEAM...
BUT IT HAD BEEN DISBANDED.
SIGH...
MUSCLES EVERYWHERE
THAT'S NOT EXACTLY A PROMISING START AT A NEW SCHOOL.
...

YAOI... GAME CLUB...?
ホモゲ部
YAOI GAME CLUB
ASSEMBLE HERE, ALL YE GAME-LOVERS!!
HEY.
HIS NAME WAS FUJIOKA KOYOMI.

WANT TO JOIN OUR CLUB?!
RIP
WHOA!
I IMMEDIATELY AGREED TO JOIN.
EVERYTHING ABOUT THIS IS COMPLETELY RIDICULOUS.
IT'S NOT A SPORTS TEAM, SO WHY ARE THEY ALL MUSCLE-BOUND MEAT-HEADS?
DON'T ASK ME.
HMM.
SORRY.
AT FIRST, FUMIO KNEW NOTHING AT ALL ABOUT YAOI GAMES...
BUT AS HE SPENT MORE TIME TALKING WITH KOYOMI AND THE OTHER CLUB MEMBERS...
HE FELL DEEPER AND DEEPER INTO THAT WORLD.

IN RETROSPECT...
SOMETIMES THEY PLAYED YAOI GAMES TOGETHER AND TALKED.
IT WAS HONESTLY HEARTWARMING TO WATCH THE CLUB MEMBERS GROW UP, BOUND TOGETHER BY THEIR LOVE OF YAOI GAMES.
SOMETIMES THEY PUSHED FUMIO TOO FAR, AND A FIGHT WOULD BREAK OUT.
IT REALLY WAS A STORY OF PEOPLE LIVING LIFE TO THE FULLEST AND LOVING EVERY MINUTE.
TALES OF HIDE
STARE
SENSEI! I'D LIKE TO PROPOSE A CLUB ACTIVITY!
COMPLETELY HOOKED WITHOUT REALIZING IT. →
SNIFF

HMMM..
HEH HEH! HOW DO YOU LIKE IT, YOZORA-SEMPAI?
RATTLED
?!
URK!
UM...
HMPH.
HEE!
NOT BAD, I GUESS.
ARE YOU FREE LATER TODAY?

藤岡
Fujioka
ザァァァ
SHAAAAA
I-I'VE NEVER INVITED ANYONE TO MY ROOM BEFORE.
THERE'S... UH...
SOMETHING I WANT TO TELL YOU. WILL YOU LISTEN...?
WHAT IS IT?

KOYOMI BEGAN TELLING ME ABOUT HIS PAST.
WITH HIS VOICE SHAKING...

BECAUSE OF A DEVASTATING EXPERIENCE IN HIS YOUTH...

HE WAS NEVER ABLE TO GET CLOSE TO OTHER PEOPLE...
ANY MORE THAN WAS ABSOLUTELY UNAVOIDABLE.

KOYOMI...
THANKS FOR TRUSTING ME WITH THIS.
F-FUMIO ...!
THUD
THAT WAS THE FIRST TIME KOYOMI CALLED ME BY MY FIRST NAME.
THAT WAS WHEN WE TRULY BECAME FRIENDS.
CLASP
I'M SO GLAD.
YEAH ...!

SMOOCH
ちゅ
RATTLE
KISSY

WHAAAAAAAAA-
AAAAAAAAAAAA-
AAAAAAAAAAAA
????!!!!
MMM
...
UNNNH
...
♥
NIBBLE
SMOOCH
KIS
AH...
MN!

staff
turuyama wataru
oryboard
hayashi junpei
MMM ...!!
Fin
UH...
DUMB-FOUNDED
THOSE TWO HOURS JUST *FLEW BY*, DIDN'T THEY?
EARNEST
THANK YOU FOR SHARING SUCH A MASTERPIECE WITH US.
NO, NO. THE PLEASURE WAS ALL RIKA'S.

......
UH... I HAVE A QUESTION, RIKA.
FSSH
WHAT IS IT, SEMPAI?
AT THE END... YOU KNOW...
W-
WHY DID FUMIO AND KOYOMI...
K...
KISS?
YOU'RE ASKING ABOUT THEM KISSING?
Y-YEAH.
DON'T SAY IT SO BLUNTLY.
NATURALLY...
THEY KISSED BECAUSE...
THEIR EMOTIONS WERE OUT OF CONTROL!
HUH?

B-BUT THEY WERE *FRIENDS*, WEREN'T THEY?!
STAND
YOU'RE SAYING... FRIENDS K-KISS?!
CERTAINLY!
IF THEY GET EXCITED ENOUGH, THEY SMOOCH AWAY.
THAT'S WHAT HUMANS DO.
BUT WHY WOULD *FRIENDS* DO THAT...?!
RIKA WOULD ARGUE THAT IT'S *BECAUSE* THEY'RE FRIENDS...
THAT WHEN THEY DO IT, IT'S WITH SUCH INTENSE PASSION!
......

THAT'S WEIRD!
IT'S NOT WEIRD IN THE SLIGHTEST!
THAT'S THE NATURAL ORDER OF THINGS!
CRACK
IT DOESN'T MATTER IF THEY'RE "FRIENDS"...
OR BOTH MEN...
YOU SMOOCH AND DO DIRTY THINGS WITH SOMEONE YOU LOVE!
CLENCH
WHOOSH

......
FWUMP...

I-I SEE...
FRIENDS KISS EACH OTHER...

GLOW
CLAP
CLAP
DON'T GO AROUND SAYING IT DOESN'T MATTER IF IT'S TWO MEN...!
AND STOP CLAPPING, YUKIMURA.

TMP
I GUESS...
YOU WERE RIGHT ABOUT IT BEING BAD TO JUDGE OUT OF PREJUDICE.
AH!
...
SO YOU'RE EMBRACING THE WORLD OF YAOI FANDOM--!!!
GRAB
IDIOT!
NO, I AM NOT!
HMPH! WHATEVER.
I'M JUST SAYING YAOI GAME CLUB WAS PRETTY GOOD!
WHA ...?
NO WAY...
BUT ANYTHING TOO WEIRD GETS VETOED.
ALWAYS GETS CHEWED OUT FOR PLAYING HENTAI GAMES.

SMIRK
PAT
......
IF YOU'VE GOT ANY MORE GOOD MOVIES LIKE THAT, BRING THEM WITH YOU.
FLICK

OF COURSE!
BUT I VETO ANYTHING *TOO* WEIRD.

......

FSSSHT

STRETCH
STRETCH
STRETCH
MMM...!

THE GAME I PLAYED TODAY WAS PRETTY FUN.
OH, REALLY...?

SO SHE WAS PLAYING A HENTAI GAME IN THE BACK...
I THINK I WON'T COMMENT ON THE FACT THAT THE CHARACTER LOOKS JUST LIKE KOBATO.

......
FLICK

THAT REMINDS ME-- WE WON'T BE USING THE CLUB ROOM...
FOR THE REST OF THE SEMESTER.
OH, RIGHT! I REMEMBER THAT COMING UP.
I COMPLETELY FORGOT.
WHAT A PIECE OF WORK.
SIGH...
REPORT FOR TODAY'S NEIGHBORS CLUB ACTIVITY...
SOMETHING STIRRED INSIDE YOZORA AFTER WE WATCHED A BOYS' LOVE ANIME.
ALSO, RIKA GOT A MAKEOVER.
YET ANOTHER UNIMPRESSIVE OUTCOME.

WHAT'S THE MATTER, KODAKA?
NAH. IT'S NOTHING.
BURP
OH MY!

WHAT'S KOBATO-CHAN BEEN UP TO?

HAVING A STARING CONTEST WITH HER DESK.

UM... WHAT?!

SHUT
???

SMIRK
SO THERE'S STILL *ONE* LITTLE LAMB TO BE WORRIED ABOUT...

TO BE CONTINUED!

MWA HA! AT LAST,
A COMRADE IN ARMS!
BUT IF RIKA DOESN'T CHOOSE
HER NEXT SELECTION WISELY,
IT'LL ALL BE FOR NOTHING!
CALM DOWN, SHIGUMA RIKA...!
MY LITTLE WILLY
CAN'T BE THIS CUTE
IS A TRUE MASTERPIECE, BUT
ALAS, ONLY THE 18+ VERSION
HAS BEEN RELEASED...
IT CAME CRAWLING!
NYARUO-SAN
IS A MONSTER SERIES,
SO IT SHOULD BE HELD IN
RESERVE UNTIL LATER...
SOMETHING ACCESSIBLE AND
SOFTCORE...
MAYBE SHE'D APPRECIATE
SHAKY KIDS!

MWA HA HA!
NO WEIRD ONES, ALL RIGHT!

THIS IS THE STORY...
KWHAM
OF WHAT HAPPENED BETWEEN THE TIME WHEN HASEGAWA KODAKA ARRIVED AT MY SCHOOL...
NEIGHBORS CLUB
BECOME SOMEONE WHO, REGARDLESS OF THE SITUATION,
OFTEN CREATES MEMORIES WITH OTHER MEMBERS,
REFINES BOTH BODY AND MIND,
AMASSES THE TRUST OF THE PEOPLE,
GRASPS THE SITUATION AND ADAPTS ACCORDINGLY,
ESTABLISHES GOOD RELATIONS WITH NEIGHBORS, AND
ENERGIZES YOUR FELLOW MAN UNTIL THE DAY WE DEPART.
NOW RECRUITING!
AND THE TIME THE NEIGHBORS CLUB WAS CREATED.

Haganai
I don't have many friends

IT ALL STARTED A LONG TIME AGO, REALLY.

I USED TO HAVE A CLOSE FRIEND.
HIS NAME WAS TAKA.

BUT HE DISAPPEARED TEN YEARS AGO.
AFTER THAT... LET'S JUST SAY THAT A LOT OF THINGS ABOUT MY LIFE WENT WRONG.

WHILE TRYING FILL THE VOID WHERE TAKA HAD BEEN...

I MADE ALL KINDS OF MISTAKES.

UNTIL THE DAY TAKA TRANSFERRED BACK.
LIVE NIKO
ONE SCREW-UP LED TO ANOTHER...
AND ANOTHER...
TYPE TYPE
BRAGS ON HER BLOG ABOUT COMMITTING A CRIME.
FLAMED ON SOCIAL MEDIA.
UPLOADS COSPLAY PHOTO TO THE INTERNET.
AND ANOTHER ...
......
GRRR
FLAIL
FLAIL

I'D GIVEN UP ON EVEN TRYING TO LEAD A HAPPY TEENAGE LIFE.
Haganai
I don't have many friends
CONNECT
TIME BEGINS MOVING AGAIN

......
TAKA ...!

ONE MONTH LATER...

2—5

......

TREMBLE
TREMBLE

THAT JERK!
HE STILL HASN'T FIGURED IT OUT!!
GAH
GASP
GLANCE
GLANCE
TMP
TMP

SIGH...
THERE'S NO ONE HERE, RIGHT...?
THAT'S A RELIEF...

SHUT
A WHOLE MONTH HAD PASSED SINCE TAKA CAME TO MY SCHOOL.
BUT HE STILL HADN'T REALIZED THAT I WAS SORA, AND...
I HAVEN'T EVEN HAD A CHANCE TO TALK WITH HIM IN PRIVATE.

ON TOP OF ALL THIS, TAKA MADE SUCH A HORRIBLE FIRST IMPRESSION WHEN HE ARRIVED...

EVERYONE IN CLASS HAS BEEN COMPLETELY TERRIFIED OF HIM.

CAN I BORROW YOUR TEXT-BOOK?
SMILE

THEY ALL ASSUMED HE WAS SOME KIND OF THUG, AND TRIED THEIR BEST TO AVOID HIM.
P-PLEASE DON'T HURT ME!
WHICH MEANT THAT I HAD TO FOLLOW SUIT AND BIDE MY TIME.

I REALLY DO WANT TO TALK TO HIM, BUT...I CAN'T JUST ACT LIKE NOTHING'S CHANGED.
KODAKA'S DESK
FRUSTRATED
HEY...
WHAT DO YOU THINK, TOMO-CHAN?
......

I THINK IT'S MY FAULT TOO...
HER "AIR FRIEND."
NO WAY!
I DON'T EVEN KNOW HOW TO START A CONVERSATION WITH SOMEONE!
A FICTIONAL PERSON YOZORA INVENTED AFTER A CERTAIN SOMETHING THAT HAPPENED IN MIDDLE SCHOOL.
I JUST TOLD YOU!
I'M DOING MY BEST TO TRY AND GET HIM TO TALK TO ME!
SHE NEVER TRULY BELIEVED TOMO-CHAN EXISTED, OF COURSE.
I'VE MADE SURE TO BE RIGHT BY HIM...
WHEN HE COMES TO SCHOOL...
OR SOMETIMES WHEN HE GOES TO HIS LOCKER TO GET SOMETHING.
BUT WHEN THINGS GOT TOO FRUSTRATING, SHE WOULD THROW HERSELF INTO THE ROLE OF A NORMAL HIGH SCHOOL GIRL CHATTERING AWAY WITH A FRIEND-- LIKE ANYONE WITH A NORMAL OFFLINE LIFE WOULD.

HA HA!
COME ON, DON'T TEASE ME!
THE POOR GIRL...!
OH, RIGHT! TOMO-CHAN, WHAT WERE YOU SAYING WHEN--
KWHAM

UH--
ACK!

THIS IS THE WORST-CASE SCENARIO.

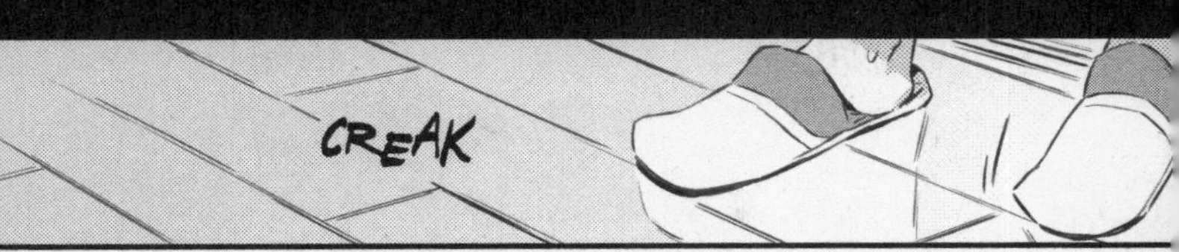

WHY DO I HAVE SUCH HORRIBL LUCK?

I DIDN'T EXPECT ANYONE TO WALK IN WHILE I WAS CHEERFULLY BLATHERING TO MYSELF.

AND OF ALL PEOPLE...
SHE'S GLARING AT ME.
WHY DID IT HAVE TO BE HIM...?!

SCRATCH
SCRATCH
WHY DID IT HAVE TO BE TAKA...?!
BLUSH
GULP
THIS IS BAD.
UH, EXCUSE ME.
VERY BAD.
THIS IS BEYOND BAD.
WHAT'LL I DO IF HE THINKS I'M SOME KIND OF WEIRDO...?!
UM...

S-SO...
CAN YOU SEE GHOSTS OR SOMETHING?
HUH?

WHA...?
THAT WAS THE FIRST CONVERSATION I'D HAD WITH TAKA IN TEN YEARS.

2-5

SINCE KODAKA SHOWED NO SIGNS OF COMING ANY CLOSER...
HEY, HEY!
YOZORA ADMITTED THAT SHE'D BEEN TALKING TO HER "FRIEND." SHE EVEN MADE SURE TO MENTION HOW PRETTY TOMO-CHAN WAS.
WHAT THE HELL'S SHE GOING ON ABOUT?
AARGH, I REALLY SCREWED UP!

I WAS SERIOUSLY ANGRY AT MYSELF.
HUNH... I JUST NOTICED. YOU'RE THAT NEW KID WHO'S ALWAYS ALONE.
I'VE BEEN HERE FOR A MONTH, SO I'M NOT EXACTLY *NEW* ANYMORE.

OKAY, HE DOESN'T LIKE BEING CALLED "NEW KID."
HMM...

WHAT'S YOUR NAME?
HASEGAWA KODAKA.
HUH? I WAS TRYING TO ASK WHAT I SHOULD CALL HIM, BUT HE JUST GAVE ME HIS FULL NAME!

AAARGH!
WHY CAN'T HE JUST UNDERSTAND WHAT I'M TRYING TO SAY...?!!
I AL-READY KNEW THAT!

SHOULD I JUST CALL HIM "TAKA" AND SURPRISE HIM?
WOULD THAT MAKE HIM REALIZE I'M SORA...?
BUT... WHAT IF IT DOESN'T?

......

I DECIDED THAT I'D JUST CALL HIM "KODAKA"...
UNTIL WE WERE ACTUALLY FRIENDS AGAIN.

GOTCHA, KODAKA.

JUST LIKE THAT, SHE THINKS WE'RE ON A FIRST-NAME BASIS...?

ALL I WANTED WAS SOME MORE TIME TOGETHER.

GRIN
?

STAFF ROOM
EX-CUSE ME!

OF COURSE!
ALL I HAVE TO DO IS START A CLUB!

RUSTLE
A CLUB JUST FOR ME AND TAKA!

THE NAVE OF THE CHURCH AND THE LOUNGE WERE ALMOST ALWAYS FREE...
SO WHEN THE CLASSROOM OR LIBRARY GOT TOO LOUD FOR ME TO RELAX...
I'D GO TO ONE OF THOSE SPOTS FOR PEACE AND QUIET.

WHAT I WAS LOOKING FOR...
WAS COMMON ROOM 4 IN THE CHAPEL.
I THOUGHT I MIGHT BE ABLE TO USE IT FOR A CLUB FOR ME AND KODAKA.
THIS IS IT!

THE NUN IN CHARGE OF THE ROOM...
IS A LITTLE GIRL FROM NORTHERN EUROPE NAMED TAKAYAMA MARIA.
I'VE NEVER MET HER BEFORE, BUT I'M SURE SHE'S A SWEET GIRL.
I DON'T HAVE ANYTHING AGAINST KIDS.
KNOC KNOC
OPEN
EXCUSE ME--!!
?!
HUH ...?

YAWN
SO CUTE...!
UM...
I'M MIKAZUKI YOZORA. CLASS 2-5, SEAT 31.
FWIP
I HAVE A REQUEST FOR TAMAYAMA MARIA-SENSEI.

NO!
HUH?

UH, I'D LIKE TO START A NEW CLUB.
MAY WE USE THIS ROOM?
SHOULD I PUNCH HER?
MORON!!
MORON!!
RES-TRAIN YOUR-SELF!
TOMO
BULGE
NOT MY PROBLEM, MORON!
GRRROWL
RUSTLE
UHHH...
AWW. SHE'S JUST IN A BAD MOOD 'CAUSE SHE'S HUNGRY.
HEH
SHE'S SUCH A KID--! ♡
LET'S TRY SOME OLD-FASHIONED BRIBERY!
UM, HERE. YOU CAN HAVE THIS.
IS IT GOOD?!

HOVER
HOVER
HOVER
I'M PRETTY SURE I HAVE SOME CHOCOLATE IN HERE...
......
WHERE IS IT...?
GIMME!
WHACK
FOUND IT!
PUGOBYA ?!
CRACK
ACK!

CRUMPLE
WAA-AAA-AAA-AAA-AAH!!
THAT LOOKED LIKE IT HURT...
YOU SAID YOU WERE GONNA GIVE ME SOMETHING GOOD AND THEN YOU HIT ME!
WHY'D YOU HIT ME?! MORON! MORON! POOP!!
......
I DON'T HAVE TIME TO WASTE HERE...!
...
GULP

HEH! IDIOT!
THAT'S WHY I GAVE YOU A SMACK! YOU SHOULD BE GRATEFUL.
I DON'T HAVE A CHOICE.
I'LL HAVE TO CHANGE THE PLAN.
"WHO-SOEVER SHALL SMITE THEE...
"ON THY RIGHT CHEEK...
"TURN TO HIM THE OTHER ALSO. THUS SAITH THE LORD."
I SAID NO SUCH THING.
WHAAAA?!
SMACK
SO I'LL SLAP THE LEFT ONE, TOO!
OWW!

WAAAAAAH!
SNIFF...
NOW...
MARIA-SENSEI.
STOMP
QUIET
HYAU!
THERE'S A GOOD GIRL.
Common Room 4
"AND THE LORD CONTINUED..."

THE NEXT DAY.
2-5
SIGH...
GREAT. I BULLIED A LITTLE GIRL.
BIIIING
BOOOONG
I'LL GIVE HER SOME CANDY LATER.
BEEEENG
BOOOONG
I REALLY HAVE TO STOP GETTING ALL CARRIED AWAY IN WHATEVER ROLE I'M PLAYING...

WELL, NO USE CRYING OVER SPILLED MILK.
INDEED.
SLAM
THERE'S SOMETHING LOT MORE URGENT TO TAKE CARE OF!

COME
WITH ME,
KODAKA.

THAT'S
RIGHT.

THIS IS OUR CLUB!
I'VE CALLED IT THE NEIGHBORS CLUB.
Common Room 4
ITS OFFICIAL PURPOSE IS "TO MAKE FRIENDS"...
NEIGHBORS CLUB
BECOME SOMEONE WHO, REGARDLESS OF THE SITUATION,
OFTEN CREATES MEMORIES WITH OTHER MEMBERS,
REFINES BOTH BODY AND MIND,
AMASSES THE TRUST OF THE PEOPLE,
GRASPS THE SITUATION AND ADAPTS ACCORDINGLY,
ESTABLISHES GOOD RELATIONS WITH NEIGHBORS, AND
ENERGIZES YOUR FELLOW MAN UNTIL THE DAY WE DEPART.
NOW RECRUITING!
BUT...
THE REAL OBJECTIVE IS TO MAKE IT POSSIBLE...

FOR MIKAZUKI YOZORA...
AND HASEGAWA KODAKA--

FOR SORA AND TAKA TO BE FRIENDS AGAIN.
HEE!

THIS IS WHERE MY REAL TEENAGE LIFE BEGINS!

Common Room 4
THEN THERE WAS A HITCH.
KNOCK
KNOCK
LOOKS LIKE THEY'RE ALREADY STARTING TO ROLL IN.
NO WAY.
NOW, JOKES ASIDE...
I'LL JUST GO HAVE A WORD WITH THIS INTRUDER.

THIS IS THE NEIGHBORS CLUB, RIGHT?

I'D LIKE TO JOIN.

THE STORY HAD ONLY JUST BEGUN, AND IT WAS ALREADY TAKING A DIFFERENT PATH THAN I HAD PLANNED...

SHINE
THIS IS WHERE MY REAL TEENAGE LIFE BEGINS!
SHINE
EVEN I HAVE MOMENTS LIKE THAT OCCASIONALLY.

IN THE NEXT VOLUME...
MIIN
MIIN
MIIN
A MYSTERIOUS NUN IS WATCHING KODAKA...!

SO THERE'S STILL ONE LITTLE LAMB TO BE WORRIED ABOUT...
SMIRK

As a new character--a beautiful nun
who's older than she looks(?!)--arrives,
it seems like a new storm is on the horizon for the Neighbors Club!

HAGANAI: I DON'T HAVE MANY FRIENDS VOL. 8

COMING SOON!

BURP
OH MY!

Random Additional Material (Reunion)

I...
I FORCED MYSELF TO GO TO A SALON...
FOR THE FIRST TIME IN TEN YEARS!
WHAT DID YOU DO IN THOSE TEN YEARS?

I CUT IT MYSELF.
SO THAT'S WHY SHE KEPT IT SO LONG...
THAT'S AMAZING.

BUT WHY ARE STYLISTS SO CHATTY?
WHAT HIGH SCHOOL?
WHAT CLUB?
GOT A BOY-FRIEND?
MY PERSONAL LIFE HAS NOTHING TO DO WITH YOU!

DID YOU TRY TO DYE YOUR HAIR YOURSELF? (LOL)
STYLIST →
I COULDN'T AGREE MORE.

Afterword!

It's time to celebrate!
We've made it to volume 7!

Picking up where the last volume left off, Yozora sort of hogged the spotlight this time. How was it? I hope you all enjoyed it! We've got a new character coming up, and the other characters will all have more screen time next volume--although, Sena might get some more focus. All right! See you in volume 8!

Itachi

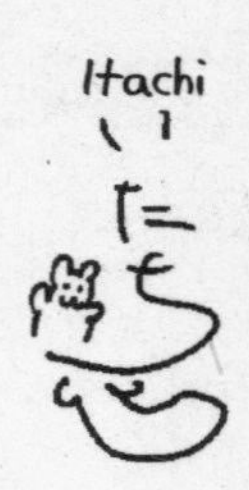

Staff
Murayama-san
Joe-san
Thanks for everything!

In lieu of comments by Yomi Hirasaka, the original creator, the Neighbors Club are going to provide a bit of commentary for each chapter!

Club Activity Log 29: Reunion

MAN, I HAD NO IDEA YOU WERE SORA. YOU REALLY SURPRISED ME!

WELL, *YOU* SURPRISED *ME*, TOO! I THOUGHT YOU'D HAVE MORE OF A REACTION THAN BEING SURPRISED! BUT WHATEVER. H-HOW DO YOU LIKE MY NEW HAIRCUT...?

O-OH, UH... WELL... I KNOW LONG BLACK HAIR IS WAY MORE POPULAR ON MOE CHARACTERS, BUT PERSONALLY, I CAN'T SAY I DISLIKE IT THIS WAY...

CAN'T YOU JUST GIVE ME A STRAIGHTFORWARD COMPLIMENT?!

Club Activity Log 30: Pouf

RIKA APOLOGIZES, SENA-SEMPAI. SHE LET HERSELF GET CARRIED AWAY.

YEAH...I DON'T KNOW WHAT TO SAY. SORRY, I GUESS.

MY DEEPEST APOLOGIES, ANEGO SENA...

UGH! I TOLD YOU IT DOESN'T MATTER ANYMORE! JUST FORGET ABOUT IT!

BUT SO MANY PEOPLE SAW YOU WITH THAT HAIR--PEOPLE AT SCHOOL AND ON THE BUS, AND EVEN YOUR DAD! EVEN THOUGH IT WAS *YOU* AS THE BUTT OF THE JOKE, MEAT, I FEEL LIKE I CROSSED A LINE. THAT WAS REALLY CRUEL OF M

INDEED. IF THAT HAD HAPPENED TO RIKA, SHE WOULD HAVE HAD LIFELONG TRAUMA. RIKA BELIEVES THAT IF IT HAD BEEN HER, MERELY RECALLING THE INCIDENT WOULD MAKE HER WANT TO DIE FROM SHAME.

I COULDN'T AGREE MORE. MEAT, HOW DO YOU GO ON LIVING AFTER ALL THAT

ARE...ARE YOU GUYS TRYING TO ADD SALT TO THE WOUND ON PURPOSE...?

OH, SHE FIGURED IT OUT.

Activity Log 31: Yaoi Game Club

YAOI GAME CLUB... IT WAS A PRETTY GOOD MOVIE...

IF YOU LIKED THE MOVIE, RIKA CAN LEND YOU THE 18+ RATED GAME! THERE ARE TONS OF FAMOUS DIRTY SCENES THAT WEREN'T INCLUDED IN THE ANIME.

UH, THAT'S OKAY.

THAT'S TOO BAD. OH, WELL. HOW DO YOU LIKE RIKA'S MAKEOVER WITH HER HAIR PULLED BACK AND HER GLASSES OFF?

IT'S CUTE.

DON'T GIVE SUCH BLUNT COMPLIMENTS!

Haganai CONNECT: Time Begins Moving Again

IT'S EMBARRASSING, SO DON'T READ IT! THAT'S ALL.

Haganai I don't have many friends GOLDEN VER.
It Happened One Summer
DID MARIA EAT ALL OF THIS?
YES. IT PAINED ME TO DO IT, BUT I FORCED HER TO EAT IT ALL.
FORCED HER?!
I NOW UNDERSTAND HOW HASHIBA HIDEYOSHI FELT WHEN EXECUTING MANPUKU-MARU.
UH... REALLY?
MANPUKU-MARU WAS THE ELDEST SON OF AZAI NAGAMASA, WHO WAS HIMSELF KILLED BY NOBUNAGA.
UNDER ORDERS FROM NOBUNAGA, HIDEYOSHI CRUCIFIED THE BOY...
AT THE TENDER AGE OF TEN.
I GUESS...
MANPUKU-MARU MUST'VE CRIED LIKE THAT TOO.
YUKI-MURA...
DID YOU FEED MARIA?
YES, SIR.
I MADE SURE TO FOLLOW YOUR INSTRUCTIONS TO THE LETTER.
WHAT DID YOU FEED HER?
A BODY-BUILDING SUPPLE-MENT.

I DUN THINK THAZ GUNNA WERK.
REALLY, SIR?

SEVEN SEAS ENTERTAINMENT PRESENTS

VOLUME 7

art by ITACHI / story by YOMI HIRASAKA / character designs by BURIKI

TRANSLATION
Ryan Peterson
ADAPTATION
Ysabet Reinhardt MacFarlane
LETTERING
Roland Amago
LAYOUT
Bambi Eloriaga-Amago
COVER DESIGN
Nicky Lim
PROOFREADER
Shanti Whitesides
MANAGING EDITOR
Adam Arnold
PUBLISHER
Jason DeAngelis

HAGANAI: I DON'T HAVE MANY FRIENDS VOL. 7

Edited by MEDIA FACTORY.
First published in Japan in 2012 by KADOKAWA CORPORATION, Tokyo.
English translation rights reserved by Seven Seas Entertainment, LLC.
under the license from KADOKAWA CORPORATION, Tokyo.

ISBN: 978-1-626920-35-4

Printed in Canada

First Printing: June 2014

10 9 8 7 6 5 4 3 2 1

READING DIRECTIONS

This book reads from ***right to left***, Japanese style. If this is your first time reading manga, you start reading from the top right panel on each page and take it from there. If you get lost, just follow the numbered diagram here. It may seem backwards at first, but you'll get the hang of it! Have fun!!

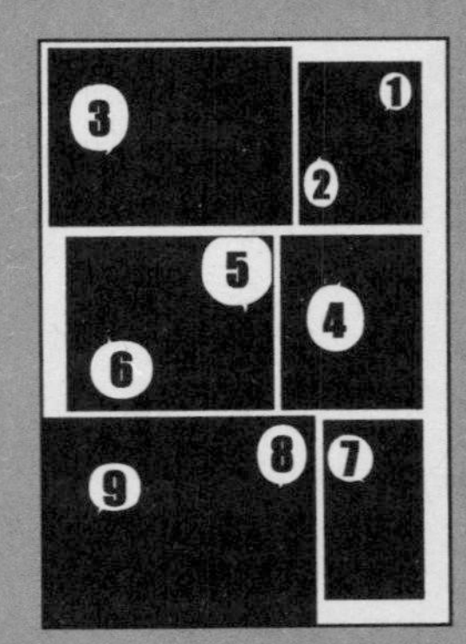